# Tallinn

## Travel Guide
## 2024

Your Ultimate Travel Companion For
2024 And Beyond

## Monica Friend

*Copyrighted Material*

Copyright©Monica Friend2023

All right reserved.

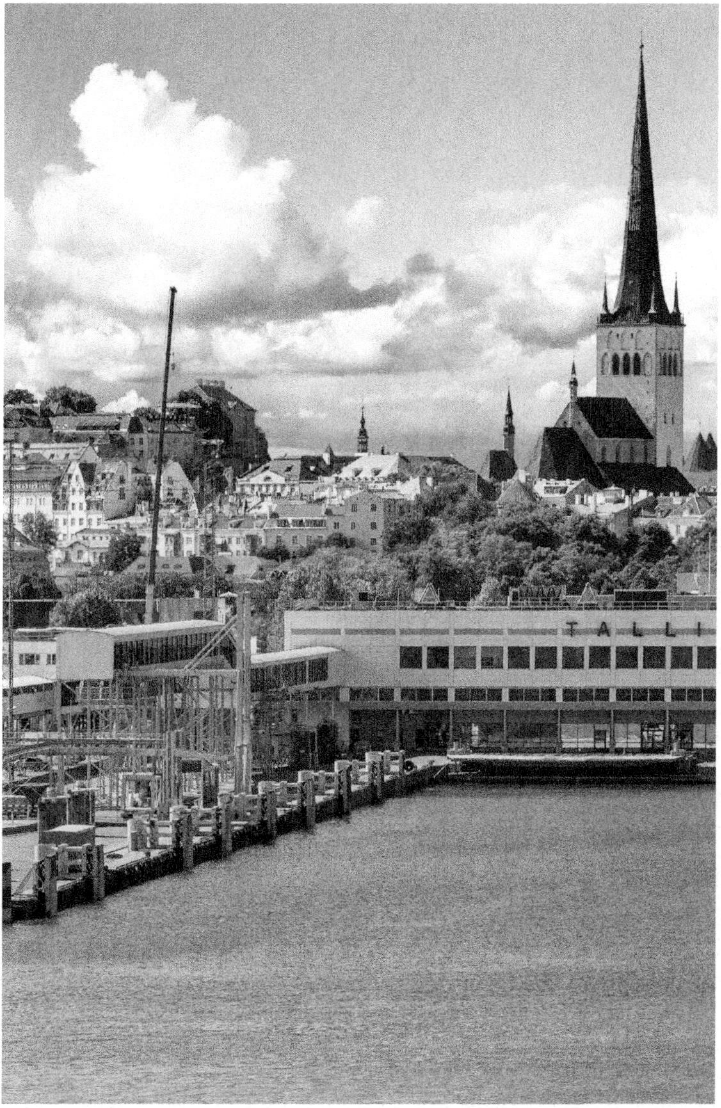
TALLI

*Copyrighted Material*

# Content

Introduction
About Tallinn
    History And Cultures
    Geography And Climate
    Getting There
    Getting Around
Planning Your Trip
    When To Visit
    Visa And Passport Requirements
    Language Spoken
    Things To Pack
    Tips For Staying Safe
Top Attractions
    Town Hall Square
    The Town Hall
    Alexander Nevsky Cathedral
    St. Olaf's Church
    Toompea Castle
    Kadriorg Palace
    Kadriorg Park
    Tallinn Zoo
    Rocca al Mare Open Air Museum

*Copyrighted Material*

    Tallinn Children's Museum
    Lennusadam Seaplane Harbour
Food And Drinks
    Traditional Estonian food
    Recommended Restaurants
    Estonian bars and cafés
Things To Do
Recommended Hotels
Day Trip From Tallinn
    Day Trip from Tallinn to Lahemaa National Park
    Day Trip From Tallinn To Pärnu
    Day Trip from Tallinn to Tartu
Your 5-Day Itinerary
    DAY 1
    DAY 2
    Day 3
    Day 4
    DAY 5
Conclusion
Travel planner

# Map

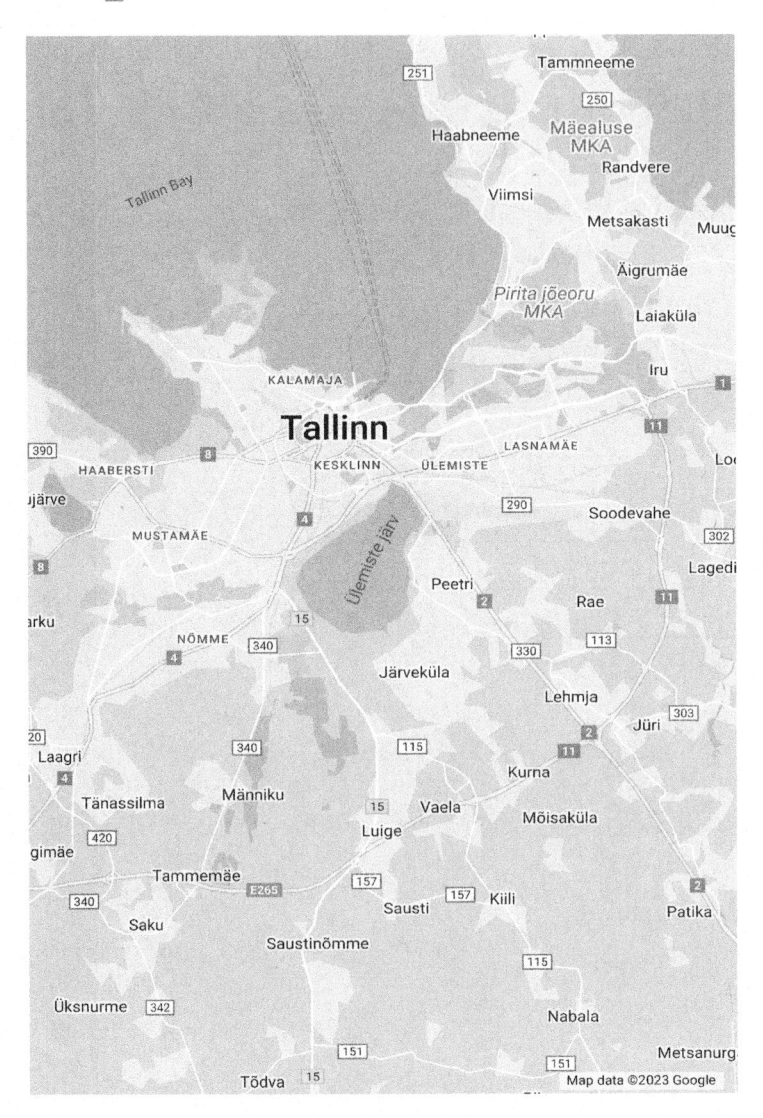

*Copyrighted Material*

# Introduction

In the heart of the Baltics lies a city that truly captured my heart, Tallinn, Estonia. Here, history whispers through cobblestone streets and the future gleams in glass skyscrapers. As I strolled through Tallinn's Old Town, I felt like a time traveler, transported to the days of knights and merchants. Each step echoed with centuries of stories, and every corner held a new tale. Medieval walls silently guarded ancient secrets.

Yet, Tallinn isn't just confined to its past. Beyond these walls, a dynamic metropolis thrives, embracing the future. The modern skyline, adorned with glass and steel, tells a different story, one of ambition and innovation. Tallinn beautifully blends the old and the new, offering a unique experience for every traveler.

In this guide, I invite you to explore Tallinn's history, savor its culinary delights, immerse yourself in its culture, and experience the warm hospitality of its people. Whether you're a history enthusiast or a food lover, Tallinn has something special for you.

But this guide isn't just about places; it's about experiences that will linger in your heart. Discover hidden gems in the charming Kadriorg district, enjoy a warm drink in a cozy café while snowflakes dance outside, and witness the beauty of the sunset over the Baltic Sea.

***Copyrighted Material***

Tallinn isn't just a destination; it's an emotion waiting to be felt. It's the excitement of discoveries, the warmth of shared laughter, and the nostalgia of timeless stories. Here, you'll create your memories and tales to cherish.

Join me on this unforgettable journey through Tallinn, where every street, square and smile has a story. Let's make memories together and uncover the magic of Tallinn, Estonia, one page at a time.

Welcome to Tallinn.

*Copyrighted Material*

# About Tallinn

## History And Cultures

Tallinn, Estonia's capital, effortlessly fuses its rich history with a modern and vibrant atmosphere. Its origins date back to the early medieval era, and its streets are a living testament to the stories that have shaped its culture.

Tallinn's story began in the 13th century, when Danish, German, and Swedish crusaders established it. Positioned strategically on the Baltic Sea, it became a sought-after trading hub. The enchanting Old Town, recognized as a UNESCO World Heritage Site, lovingly preserves the city's medieval charm, featuring well-preserved city walls, cobblestone streets, and striking Gothic architecture.

Tallinn, much like the rest of Estonia, experienced a complex 20th-century history. It was part of the Russian Empire, briefly independent post-World War I, and then occupied by both the Soviet Union and Nazi Germany during World War II. After the war, Estonia was once again incorporated into the Soviet Union. However, in 1991, Tallinn and the nation as a whole regained their independence, marking a significant turning point in their history.

Following independence, Tallinn has undergone a remarkable renaissance. It celebrates its rich cultural heritage while eagerly embracing modern advancements. The city's dedication to preserving its history is evident in its well-preserved medieval architecture and numerous museums dedicated to Estonian culture and history.

Tallinn's culture is a unique blend of Estonian traditions and influences from its neighbors. The Estonian Song Festival, held every five years, shines a spotlight on the nation's passion for choral music. Traditional folk festivals like Jaanipäev (Midsummer's Day) offer a glimpse into Estonian folklore.

Tallinn is also renowned for its digital prowess and is often dubbed the "Silicon Valley of Europe" due to its innovative e-government initiatives. In 2005, Estonia introduced e-residency, allowing people worldwide to become "digital residents" and establish businesses in the country.

## Geography And Climate

### Geography

Tallinn is the capital city of Estonia and is located on the northern coast of the country, along the shores of the Baltic Sea. It is known for its picturesque coastline, with the Gulf of Finland to the north. The city's geography includes a mix of historic old town areas, modern urban development, and natural green spaces, making it a unique and dynamic European capital.

Thi city is divided into unique districts, each with its own allure.

Old Town: The heart of Tallinn, Old Town, is a delightful labyrinth of historic streets and buildings from the 13th century. Town Hall Square is a vibrant gathering spot in the center.

Kadriorg: This elegant area is home to the splendid Kadriorg Palace, a baroque gem surrounded by lush gardens, and the Presidential Palace. It's a tranquil escape from the city's hustle and bustle.

Pirita: Situated along the coast, Pirita is known for its sandy beach and remnants of the 1980 Moscow Olympics sailing complex. It's a favored destination for outdoor enthusiasts.

Tallinn Bay: The city's shoreline along the Gulf of Finland offers picturesque vistas and opportunities for sailing, swimming, or leisurely strolls.

**Climate:**

Tallinn enjoys a humid continental climate with distinct seasons that enhance its charm year-round.

Spring: From April to June, mild temperatures and blossoming greenery make spring perfect for exploring Tallinn's parks and gardens.

Summer: June to August is the peak tourist season, with long sunny days and temperatures ranging from 15°C (59°F) to 22°C (72°F). It's ideal for outdoor activities and festivals.

Autumn: September to November paints the city with the vibrant hues of fall. Parks, like Kadriorg, become a breathtaking display of autumn foliage. Expect cooler weather and occasional rain.

Winter: December to February blanket Tallinn in snow, creating a magical winter wonderland. The average winter temperature is around -6°C (21°F), making it the perfect time to enjoy warm beverages in cozy cafes and experience the enchantment of Christmas markets.

## Getting There

Getting to Tallinn is a breeze, and we're here to guide you every step of the way, without any fancy jargon.

**By Air:**

If you're flying in, Tallinn Airport (TLL) is your go-to hub. It's just 4 km (2.5 miles) from downtown and handles both domestic and international flights. You'll find flights from major European cities like Amsterdam, London, and Helsinki, operated by airlines like Finnair, Ryanair, and Lufthansa. Exploring other parts of Estonia? No problem; there are domestic flights to places like Tartu and Kuressaare. Once you land, you've got car rentals, taxis, and public transport options at your fingertips. The city center is a quick 10-15-minute drive away.

**By Sea:**

If you prefer a scenic route, consider sailing into Tallinn. The Port of Tallinn, bustling with activity, welcomes cruise ships and ferries alike. Cruise enthusiasts can hop off on Baltic Sea cruises, and you'll be welcomed by Tallinn's stunning medieval Old Town. If you're coming from nearby Helsinki, Stockholm, or St. Petersburg, ferries are a convenient choice. The Tallinn-Helsinki route is especially popular and crosses the Gulf of Finland. Once you're at the port, getting to the city center is a breeze with taxis, buses, or a pleasant stroll along the waterfront.

**By Land:**

Estonia's well-kept roads make it easy to drive to Tallinn from neighboring countries like Latvia, Russia, and Finland. The E67 and E20 highways link Tallinn to other European cities.

If you're driving, just remember to follow local traffic rules (they drive on the right side of the road). Prefer buses? International bus services connect Tallinn with cities all over Europe. Lux Express and Ecolines are reliable options, offering comfy and budget-friendly rides.

## Getting Around

Exploring the enchanting streets of Tallinn is a breeze, and the city offers various ways to cater to every traveler's needs. Whether you're wandering through the historic Old Town or venturing into the modern neighborhoods, here's your essential guide to navigating Estonia's capital.

## Walking:

Tallinn's petite size and well-preserved Old Town make it a walker's paradise. Put on your comfy shoes and take a relaxed stroll along cobblestone streets flanked by centuries-old structures. As you meander, you'll stumble upon charming courtyards, cozy cafes, and captivating tales from the past. Don't forget your camera; every turn reveals a picturesque scene.

## Public Transport:(Trams and Buses)

When you need to travel longer distances within the city or explore areas beyond the Old Town, Tallinn's public transport system is both efficient and dependable. Trams and buses crisscross the city, and you can get tickets from vending machines or use the Tallinn Card. Trams, in particular, offer scenic routes along the coastline.

## Taxis:

Taxis are readily available and reasonably priced compared to many Western European cities. Most taxis use meters, but it's wise to request an estimate before your ride. Uber and Bolt (a popular ridesharing app) are also convenient choices in Tallinn.

**Biking:**

For eco-conscious travelers, Tallinn boasts an excellent network of bike lanes and rental stations. Exploring the city on two wheels is not only environmentally friendly but also allows you to reach less-explored areas easily. You can rent bicycles from various providers, and some even offer electric bikes for effortless uphill journeys.

**Ferries:**

If you're planning to discover Estonia's stunning islands, catch a ferry from Tallinn's port. The ferries to popular destinations like Saaremaa and Hiiumaa are comfortable and offer breathtaking views of the Baltic Sea. Make sure to check the ferry schedules in advance, especially during the bustling summer months.

**Driving: (Car Rentals)**

While driving in Tallinn is an option, it's usually unnecessary within the city itself. However, if you intend to explore the Estonian countryside or visit remote areas, renting a car is a convenient choice. Keep in mind that Tallinn's traffic can be heavy during rush hours, so plan your journeys accordingly.

# Planning Your Trip

## When To Visit

Tallinn, beckons with its unique charm throughout the year. Your ideal visit time depends on your tastes and interests.

### Summer (June to August):

Weather: Summer is peak season, offering warm temperatures ranging from 15°C to 22°C (59°F to 72°F).

Activities: It's perfect for outdoor adventures like exploring the historic Old Town, relaxing in parks, and basking on Baltic Sea beaches.

Festivals: Tallinn hosts various summer festivals, from music and food events to cultural celebrations.

Long Days: You'll enjoy extended daylight hours for your sightseeing pleasure.

**Spring (March to May):**

Weather: Spring is crisp and refreshing, with temperatures ranging from 2°C to 11°C (36°F to 52°F).

Nature: The city awakens with blossoming trees and flowers, ideal for leisurely strolls.

Fewer Crowds: Spring offers a quieter atmosphere compared to the bustling summer.

Easter Traditions: Experience Estonian Easter traditions, including vibrant egg painting and festive meals.

**Autumn (September to November):**

Weather: Autumn brings cooler temperatures, ranging from 8°C to 15°C (46°F to 59°F).

Fall Foliage: Enjoy the stunning autumn colors in parks and forests around Tallinn.

Cultural Events: The city hosts various cultural events and exhibitions during the fall.

Budget-Friendly: Prices for accommodations and flights are more wallet-friendly than in the summer.

**Winter (December to February):**

Weather: Expect cold weather, with temperatures between -5°C and 0°C (23°F and 32°F) and frequent snowfall.

Christmas Magic: Don't miss the enchanting Tallinn Christmas Market in the heart of the Old Town.

Cozy Vibes: Tallinn's medieval architecture and cozy cafes make it a perfect winter retreat.

Sauna Time: Immerse yourself in Estonia's sauna culture to stay warm during the chilly months.

Ultimately, your perfect Tallinn visit time hinges on your preferences. Summer offers warmth and liveliness, while spring and autumn provide a more relaxed experience. Winter embraces a cozy, festive atmosphere. Regardless of the season, Tallinn's rich history, culture, and natural beauty await, promising a captivating visit year-round.

*Copyrighted Material*

# Visa And Passport Requirements

Before you set off on your exciting trip to this lovely destination, it's crucial to know about the visa and passport rules.

## Passport Requirements:

To start, make sure your passport is current. Estonia requires your passport to be valid for at least three months beyond your planned departure date. It's a simple but vital step to ensure a smooth entry into the country.

## Visa Requirements

The good news for many travelers is that Estonia is part of the Schengen Area, which means that citizens from many countries can visit without a visa for stays of up to 90 days. Here are some key points to remember:

Visa-Free Travel: If you hold a passport from a Schengen Area member state or several other countries (like the United States, Canada, Australia, and many European nations), you won't need a visa for short visits. You can check the Estonian Ministry of Foreign Affairs website for a complete list of visa-exempt countries.

Extended Stays: If your plans involve staying in Estonia for over 90 days, such as for work or study, it's important to apply for a residence permit well in advance of your intended departure.

Business Travel: If you're traveling for business, be sure to clarify the purpose of your visit. If you plan to engage in business activities during your stay, it's a good idea to check with the Estonian embassy or consulate in your home country for specific requirements.

***Copyrighted Material***

As you prepare for your adventure in Tallinn, consider this: Estonia's history of independence and resilience reflects the spirit of its people. Standing before the medieval walls of Tallinn's Old Town, you can't help but envision the tales of merchants, knights, and explorers who once walked these charming cobblestone streets.

One traveler shared the heartwarming story of arriving in Tallinn with a nearly expired passport. The friendly customs officer reminded them of the three-month validity rule, granting them entry and a friendly reminder to renew their passport promptly.

Another adventurer recounted their journey to Tallinn for a cultural exchange program. While navigating the visa process for a more extended stay, they immersed themselves in Estonia's unique traditions and formed lasting friendships.

So, understanding the visa and passport requirements is your first step toward an unforgettable adventure in Tallinn. Ensure your passport is up to date, check the visa rules, and get ready to experience the enchantment of this captivating Baltic gem.

## Language Spoken

In Tallinn, Estonia's capital, the main language spoken is Estonian. It's the official language and is widely used in everyday life, government, education, and business. While Estonian is the primary language, you'll also encounter people conversing in English, Russian, and other languages, especially in tourist spots and among younger folks. English is particularly common in Tallinn's hospitality and tourism industries, making communication easy for English-speaking travelers.

*Copyrighted Material*

**Here are some handy travel phrases:**

1. Good morning! - Tere hommikust!
2. Good afternoon! - Tere päevast!
3. Good evening! - Tere õhtust!
4. Hello! - Tere!
5. Goodbye! - Nägemist!
6. Please - Palun
7. Thank you - Aitäh
8. Excuse me / I'm sorry - Vabandage
9. Yes - Jah
10. No - Ei
11. How much does this cost? - Kui palju see maksab?
12. Where is the restroom? - Kus on tualett?
13. I don't speak Estonian. - Ma ei räägi eesti keelt.
14. Do you speak English? - Kas sa räägid inglise keelt?
15. Can we get some help? - Saame abi?

16. The menu, please. - Menüü, palun.

17. I'm looking for a hotel. - Ma otsin hotelli.

18. I want to go to a restaurant. - Ma tahan restorani minna.

19. I want to go to the airport by bus/train. - Ma tahan bussi/rongi lennujaama.

20. Where is the nearest pharmacy? - Kus on lähim apteek?

Learning a few basics in the local language can enhance your travel experience and show respect for the local culture. Estonians generally appreciate visitors who make an effort to speak their language a bit.

*Copyrighted Material*

## Things To Pack

**Winter Packing Tips:**

Winter in Tallinn can get chilly, with temperatures ranging from +5 to -25°C. Layer up, but don't overdo it if it's warmer. Check the weather before dressing up.

Base layer: thermal wear

middle layer: shirt, jeans or trousers, sweater, woolen socks

Outer layer: overcoat, woolly hat, mittens, scarf, snow boots

Accessories: Umbrella

**Spring Packing Tips:**

Spring in Tallinn can be unpredictable, with temperatures ranging from -10°C to 25°C. Be ready for both cold and warm days.

Base layer: T-shirt, tights

Middle layer: shirt, jeans or trousers, dress or skirt, cardigan or hoodie

Outer layer: coat, scarf, boots, or rain boots

Accessories: umbrella, sunglasses

**Summer Packing Tips:**

Summers in Tallinn are pleasant, with temperatures around 15-20°C. Bring a light layer for occasional chilly breezes.

Base layer: T-shirt, swimsuit

Middle layer: shirt, jeans or trousers, shorts, summer dress or skirt, light cardigan

Outer layer: jacket, cap, or summer hat; comfortable shoes

Accessories: umbrella, sunglasses, sunscreen

*Copyrighted Material*

## Autumn Packing Tips:

Autumn is colorful but rainy, with temperatures up to 20°C initially, getting colder later on. Don't forget your raincoat.

Base layer: T-shirt, tights

Middle layer: shirt, jeans or trousers, dress or skirt, cardigan or hoodie

Outer layer: (Rain)coat, scarf, gloves, hat, comfortable footwear

Accessories: Umbrella

## General Tips:

Comfortable shoes are essential; there's no need for high heels.

If it rains, grab an umbrella from your hotel or use a raincoat.

Pack light; Tallinn has all the essentials.

Dress up for evenings out, but feel free to keep it casual.

Remember to dress respectfully for churches, theaters, and fancy restaurants.

## Tips For Staying Safe

Tallinn is generally a safe place to visit, but it's always smart to take precautions for a smooth and secure trip. Here are some vital tips to make your time in Tallinn enjoyable and safe:

Guard Your Stuff: Keep an eye on your belongings, especially in busy spots like the Old Town or on public transportation. Consider using a money belt or an anti-theft bag for added security.

Avoid Dark Areas: While Tallinn is safe at night, it's best to steer clear of poorly lit, deserted spots after dark. Stick to well-lit streets and well-traveled areas.

Watch Out for Scams: Be cautious of scams, like street vendors pushing their products aggressively. Stay skeptical of unsolicited offers or deals that seem too good to be true.

Choose Licensed Taxis: If you need a taxi, go for reputable, licensed companies or apps like Bolt. Always agree on the fare or make sure the meter is on before your ride.

Know Emergency Numbers: Familiarize yourself with local emergency numbers like 112, which connects you to police, ambulance, and fire services. English-speaking operators are available.

Follow the rules: Respect local laws, including traffic regulations. Public intoxication and disruptive behavior are not tolerated.

Use public transport: Tallinn's public transport is reliable and safe. Keep an eye on your belongings while on buses or trams, and make sure to validate your ticket.

Internet Safety: Public Wi-Fi is easy to find, but use a virtual private network (VPN) for added data security.

Health Precautions: Have travel insurance and know where the nearest medical facilities are. You can safely drink tap water in Tallinn.

Respect Local Customs: Learn a few Estonian phrases and respect the local culture. Estonians appreciate visitors who try to understand their way of life.

Nature Adventures: If you plan to explore Estonia's natural beauty, inform someone of your plans and take precautions like dressing appropriately for the weather and carrying essentials like water and maps.

Emergency Help: In case of an emergency or if you need assistance, don't hesitate to contact local authorities or your embassy.

While it's important to stay cautious, don't let safety concerns keep you from enjoying Tallinn's unique charm and culture. With a little awareness, you can have a safe and unforgettable visit to this Baltic gem.

*Copyrighted Material*

# Top Attractions

**Town Hall Square**

Town Hall Square is right in the heart of Tallinn's Old Town. This charming square, known as "Raekoja plats" in Estonian, is a must-visit when you explore Estonia's lovely capital. In this guide, we'll uncover the fascinating history, stunning architecture, and vibrant culture that make Town Hall Square a top attraction in Tallinn.

Town Hall Square dates back to the early 13th century, when Tallinn was a bustling medieval trading hub. At its center stands the remarkable Tallinn Town Hall, a symbol of civic authority for centuries. The building's Gothic architecture and the iconic "Old Thomas" weather vane are highlights of the square.

## The Town Hall

The Tallinn Town Hall is a magnificent structure that reflects the city's historical significance. Inside, you'll find ornate woodwork and historical artifacts. The Town Hall has been a witness to numerous events, from town council meetings to royal visits and weddings. It's a place where history truly comes alive.

Today, Town Hall Square is not just a historical site; it's a lively cultural hub. Throughout the year, it hosts events like Christmas markets, open-air concerts, and fairs. It's a gathering place for locals and visitors, offering a unique chance to experience Estonian traditions and celebrations.

## Alexander Nevsky Cathedral

The Alexander Nevsky Cathedral is a majestic symbol of Tallinn's rich history and stunning architecture. With its striking onion domes and intricate façade, this Orthodox cathedral offers a fascinating glimpse into the city's past and present.

Built in the late 19th century during Estonia's time under Russian rule, the cathedral was designed to showcase Russian dominance. It's named after Alexander Nevsky, a Russian medieval prince. The cathedral's architecture is a sight to behold, with gleaming onion domes and intricate patterns on its dark-red walls, reflecting Byzantine Revival style.

Inside, you'll discover a serene space adorned with Orthodox icons and flickering candles. The chants of the clergy create an atmosphere of reverence and history.

The Alexander Nevsky Cathedral sparks debate in Tallinn, seen by some as a reminder of Russian influence, while others appreciate its beauty and religious significance. This controversy adds to its intrigue, making it a must-see in Tallinn.

## St. Olaf's Church

St. Olaf's Church is one of Tallinn's oldest structures, dating back to the 12th century. Its towering spire, one of the tallest in the world during the 16th century, offers breathtaking panoramic views of Tallinn's Old Town and the Baltic Sea.

Despite enduring fires and invasions, the resilience of the Estonian people is evident in the church's multiple reconstructions. Inside, you'll find a serene space with vaulted ceilings and remarkable artwork.

Legends surround St. Olaf's Church, adding to its mystique. Some say it was built by a pirate searching for his stolen treasure, while others tell tales of a mystical maiden haunting the premises.

Usually open during the summer months. Check for current times and entrance fees.

As a place of worship, please dress respectfully.

## Toompea Castle

Toompea Castle, perched on a hill in Tallinn, symbolizes Estonia's rich heritage and enduring spirit. This iconic attraction offers not only stunning views of the city but also a captivating glimpse into the nation's history.

The castle's origins are shrouded in medieval mystery, and its architectural evolution mirrors Estonia's dynamic journey through time. Today, it houses the Estonian Parliament, the Riigikogu, making it a place where the nation's destiny is shaped.

## Kadriorg Palace

Kadriorg Palace, just a short distance from Tallinn's Old Town, is a testament to the grandeur of the past. Built by Peter the Great in the 18th century, this architectural masterpiece showcases a blend of Baroque and Rococo styles.

Step inside to explore the KUMU Art Museum, housing a diverse collection of Estonian art. The palace gardens offer a peaceful escape with lush greenery, fountains, and cultural events.

Kadriorg Palace is a living history book, narrating tales of love, war, and resilience from Russian royalty to Estonian independence.

## Kadriorg Park

Discover the enchanting Kadriorg Park in Tallinn, Estonia's vibrant capital. Commissioned by Peter the Great as a gift to his beloved wife Catherine I, this historic park is a testament to their enduring love. Explore the exquisite Kadriorg Palace, now home to the Art Museum of Estonia. Stroll through meticulously manicured gardens, enjoy the serene Swan

Pond, and savor the park's cultural delights, including open-air concerts and art exhibitions. Perfect for picnics and relaxation, Kadriorg Park offers a blend of natural beauty and cultural charm.

## Tallinn Zoo

Located in Tallinn's heart, Tallinn Zoo invites you into a world of biodiversity. Established in 1939, it's one of Northern Europe's oldest zoos, now home to over 13,000 animals from 550 species. Get up close with giraffes and playful lemurs. Experience the zoo's commitment to conservation and education. A paradise for wildlife enthusiasts, this zoo promises an unforgettable connection with the animal kingdom.

## Rocca al Mare Open Air Museum

Step back in time at Rocca al Mare Open Air Museum, a living history book on the Baltic Sea's shores. Explore traditional Estonian farmhouses, windmills, and cottages, each narrating Estonia's rural heritage. Witness artisans crafting pottery and textiles, offering authentic experiences. The museum transforms with the seasons, from lush gardens in summer to magical snow-covered landscapes in winter. A captivating journey into Estonia's past awaits.

## Tallinn Children's Museum

Ignite young minds at Tallinn Children's Museum, an educational wonderland in Estonia's capital. Dive into interactive exhibits covering science, nature, history, and art. Young adventurers can explore a replica Viking ship, while parents appreciate the museum's educational value. It's not just for kids; it's a place for the young at heart to bond over the joy of exploration.

## Lennusadam Seaplane Harbour

Embark on a maritime adventure at Lennusadam Seaplane Harbour, Tallinn's extraordinary maritime museum. Explore historic seaplanes suspended from the ceiling, revealing Estonia's aviation and naval history. Step inside a World War II submarine, the Lembit, and test your maritime skills with interactive exhibits. Outside, stroll along the boardwalk, admire Tallinn's skyline, and marvel at the colossal icebreaker Suur Tõll. Family-friendly and rich in history, it's a must-visit destination.

*Copyrighted Material*

# Food And Drinks

## Traditional Estonian food

Discover the heart of Estonian cuisine, a delightful blend of ancient traditions and regional influences from Finland, Sweden, Russia, Germany, and Latvia. The Estonian culinary journey revolves around the changing seasons, where hearty winter meals combat the cold while light and fresh summer dishes celebrate the sun-soaked harvest.

**Must-Try Estonian Delicacies:**

**Eesti Kartulisalat** (Estonian Potato Salad)

Indulge in the quintessential Estonian party dish. Eesti Kartulisalat, a medley of peas, carrots, potatoes, and cucumbers sourced from local gardens, harmoniously combined with sausages, hard-boiled eggs, and a touch of mayonnaise

**Rosolje**

Savor the nostalgia of traditional Estonian gatherings with Rosolje, a vibrant purple salad. Boiled potatoes, beetroot, herring, and pickles dance together in a creamy blend of sour cream, mayonnaise, and mustard dressing. Delightful slices of hard-boiled eggs, meat, or apples add depth to this classic Estonian creation.

## Mulgikapsad

Embark on a culinary adventure with Mulgikapsad, a beloved Estonian dish hailing from the southern region. Immerse yourself in the flavors of sour cabbage, barley groats, and tender pork, slow-cooked to perfection. This centuries-old delight captivates the senses, evolving into a culinary masterpiece over time.

## Mulgipuder

Experience the rustic charm of Mulgipuder, a traditional Estonian porridge rooted in history. This comforting dish, often made with barley, mashed potatoes, and succulent meat, enchants with its creamy texture. Modern variations include a touch of milk, creating a velvety porridge that pairs exquisitely with bacon, sautéed onions, and rye bread.

### Kiluvõileib (Sprat Sandwich)

Experience the taste of the Baltic Sea with Kiluvõileib, a cherished Estonian snack. This delectable sandwich features Estonian black bread adorned with butter or munavõi (egg butter), crowned by slices of hard-boiled egg, onions, fresh greens, and a sprat fillet sourced from the Baltic Sea. Find it at parties, festive gatherings, and restaurants across Estonia.

**Frikadellisupp** (Meatball Soup)

Indulge in Frikadellisupp, affectionately known as "meatball soup." A beloved comfort dish, it combines vegetables and meatballs, with carrots, potatoes, peas, and onions often playing starring roles. Perfect for warming up on Estonia's rainy days, it is especially favored among schoolchildren.

**Verivorst** (Blood Sausage)

Celebrate Christmas the Estonian way with Verivorst, a traditional holiday treat. Crafted from pig's blood, barley, pork, and spices, this sausage arrived in Estonia via Swedes and Latvians in the 19th century. Traditionally prepared at home, it's now readily available in stores. Pair it with cranberry jam, marinated pumpkin, sour cabbage, and sour cream for an authentic Estonian Christmas feast.

## **Pirukas** (Pastry)

Discover Pirukas, a pastry that's deeply rooted in Estonian culture. Originally made from rye flour, it offers a variety of fillings, including cabbage, salted fish, cheese, ham, and sweet options like apple-cinnamon or rhubarb. This pastry reflects the changing tastes of Estonia over time.

## **Kringel**

Join the festivities with Kringel, a Scandinavian pastry popular at parties and celebrations. This braided bread comes in sweet or savory versions, filled with delights like raisins, almonds, chocolate, cheese, ham, or even plant-based alternatives. A versatile treat, it can serve as both a main dish and a dessert.

**Kirju Koer** (Colorful Dog)

Indulge in the nostalgia of Kirju Koer, a beloved Estonian dessert cherished by kids and adults alike. Made from vanilla-flavored biscuits, marmalade cubes, cocoa powder, butter, and condensed milk, it's a delightful treat. Families often add their own unique twist, incorporating raisins, chocolate, or even a touch of rum.

**Küpsetatud Õunad** (Baked Apples)

Celebrate Estonia's love for apples with Küpsetatud Õunad, a wholesome delight. Apples are hollowed out and filled with a mixture of sugar or honey, raisins, cinnamon, and hazelnuts before being baked to perfection. Whether enjoyed on cold winter nights or sunny summer days, it's a flavorful treat.

**Vastlakukkel** (Sweet Bun)

Satisfy your sweet tooth with Vastlakukkel, a sweet bun filled with whipped cream and jam, dusted with powdered sugar. This delightful treat is a highlight of Vastlapäev, a joyous winter celebration filled with fun activities and, of course, Estonian cuisine.

Embark on a culinary journey through Estonia, where each dish tells a unique story of tradition, taste, and cherished moments shared with loved ones.

*Copyrighted Material*

## Recommended Restaurants

Top Dining Spots in Tallinn

### NOA Chef's Hall

Address: Ranna Tee 3, Tallinn, Pirita

Escape into a world of culinary wonder at NOA Chef's Hall. Enjoy a world-class dining experience with unique wine selections and impeccable service. Indulge in their multi-course tasting menu, but be prepared to spend approximately 3 hours to fully savor the experience. NOA Chef's Hall has been recognized as the best restaurant in the Baltics in 2017, 2018, 2019, and 2020.

## Restaurant 180°

Address: Staapli Street 4, Tallinn, Kalamaja, and Pelgulinn

Experience culinary excellence at Restaurant 180° by Matthias Diether in the Port Noblessner area. Renowned German head chef Matthias Diether offers a choice between the four-course "Flavours of 180 Degrees" tasting menu and the six-course "Matthias' Inspiration" tasting menu.

## Restaurant Lee

Address: Uus Street 31, Vanalinn, Tallinn, 10111

Discover the cozy charm of Restaurant Lee, located near Tallinn's Old Town walls. Enjoy classic decor with a brick and wood-clad dining room, sheepskin seating, and a welcoming garden terrace. Chef Janno Lepik celebrates Estonian culinary traditions with modern flair, sourcing ingredients from local farmers. Savor dishes like beef tartare with ash mayo, grilled quail with roasted cabbage salad, and black-bread ice cream. Don't miss their craft beer selection.

## Restaurant Härg

Address: Maakri Street 21, Tallinn, City Centre

For steak aficionados, Restaurant Härg is a must-visit. They specialize in high-quality steaks, slow-cooked meats, delicious grilled dishes, and fresh salads and juices. Their extensive wine list, using the Coravin method for many wines, perfectly complements the cuisine. Enjoy a cozy atmosphere, good music, a stylish interior, and an inviting courtyard.

## Mantel Ja Korsten Restaurant

Address: J. Poska Street, 19a, Tallinn, Kadriorg

Hidden in a charming green building, Mantel Ja Korsten Restaurant offers a unique dining experience. Explore their menu featuring swordfish, mackerel, local beetroot, and fresh cabbage. Don't miss the picanha meat, cooked on the Green Egg Grill at high temperatures. Mediterranean-inspired flavors and a selection of exciting wines await.

## Viru Burger x Volta Restaurant

Address: Tööstuse Street, 47d, Tallinn, Kalamaja, and Pelgulinn

Embrace the hip vibes of Kalamaja district at Viru Burger x VOLTA Restaurant. Enjoy high-quality burgers, house-made French fries, and groovy tunes. Opt for a delicious and healthy salad as an alternative to French fries.

## Restaurant Tuljak

Address: Pirita Tee 26e, Tallinn, Kadriorg

After a 50-year hiatus, Restaurant Tuljak is back! This stylish restaurant, nestled in iconic Soviet architecture from the 1960s, offers a large terrace, green surroundings, a pool, and an ice cream stand. The menu combines classics like herring with bonfire potatoes and curd pancakes with modern flavors, including Oriental noodle soup. Experience a blend of tradition and innovation in a dining room and terrace that can host up to 300 guests.

## Anno's Home Restaurant & Winery

Address: Poldri Street 3, Tallinn, City Centre

Anna and Erno, the passionate owners of Anno's, welcome you to their cozy restaurant for an intimate dining experience. With a seating capacity of up to 22 guests, Anno serves European cuisine made from locally sourced ingredients. Anna's culinary creations are complemented by Erno's extensive wine selection. Dining at Anno's feels just like being at home. Please note the restaurant's weekday hours: 12–3 p.m. and 6–10 p.m.

## Estonian bars and cafés

### Bakery Karjase sai

Address: Marati Street 5, Tallinn, Kopli

Karjase Sai is a small bakery located in the Põhjala Factory at the end of Kopli. They specialize in sourdough white bread, bread, and croissants. In addition to their baked goods, they offer quality coffee and natural wine, sourced from local farmers and organic producers. You can enjoy fresh pastries throughout the day, starting as early as 9 a.m.

## Pancake Counter Kooker on the Town Hall Square

Address: Raekoja Plass 1, Tallinn, Old Town

Delight in the joy of mini pancakes at Kooker, located on the historic Tallinn Town Hall Square. They make fresh dough daily using regional ingredients like milk, eggs, and butter. Don't miss their homemade jams and sauces. Kooker also serves refreshing beverages, including rhubarb lemonade and modern summer cocktails.

## Restaurant MuSu

Address: Pärnu Mnt 484, Tallinn, Nõmme

MuSu, short for "Minu" (mine) and "Sinu" (yours), reflects a place for friends and good company. Their menu offers diverse flavors from around the world, featuring Estonian, Asian, and American cuisines. The drinks menu focuses on bubbly drinks, and the wine list boasts a wide selection. The restaurant even has a play corner for the littlest guests.

## Panorama T1

Address: Peterburi Tee 2, Tallinn, 11415 Estonia

Enjoy a cozy rooftop cocktail bar with a delightful atmosphere. Partnered with a food restaurant, Panorama T1 offers a wide range of

European dishes. Plus, they have shishas for an added touch of enjoyment.

## Whisper Sister

Address: Pärnu Mnt 12, Tallinn 10148 Estonia

Step into the hidden world of Whisper Sister, a speakeasy-style bar in the heart of Tallinn. Inspired by classic cocktail bars worldwide, it promises a unique and elegant drinking experience.

## Vaat Brewery and Taproom

Address: Telliskivi Tee 60m, Tallinn 10412 Estonia

Discover an Estonian microbrewery known for its sustainability. Located in the vibrant

Telliskivi area, Vaat Brewery & Taproom offers its own beers and a thoughtfully curated selection from Estonian breweries and importers. Get a glimpse of their modern brewery from the taproom.

## Things To Do

Tallinn offers visitors stunning views and plenty of things to do. Estonians are known to be friendly and welcoming, making visiting their capital one of the most enjoyable travel experiences out there. Here are the best places you should visit in Tallinn, Estonia.

**City Mall and Historic Marvels**

Begin your journey at City Mall, a bustling hub for shopping enthusiasts located near the iconic Topia Hill. From here, explore the fascinating Seaplane Harbor Estonia Maritime Museum and delve into history at Hellmann Tower and City Wall. Discover architectural wonders at Saint Mary's Cathedral and Town Hall. Don't miss the charm of Rotermann Quarter and Telliskivi Creative City for a taste of Tallinn's creativity.

**Freedom Square**

Immerse yourself in the rich history of Freedom Square, a monument celebrating Estonia's liberation. Explore the awe-inspiring Alexander Nevsky Cathedral, the House of Parliament, and the poignant World War II memorial.

**Kadriorg Park**

Step into the serene oasis of Kadriorg Park, a masterpiece of design and nature. Marvel at the lush greenery, ancient trees, and sculptures. Enjoy open-air concerts, jogging tracks, and winter ice skating. Visit the enchanting Rose Garden in spring, a perfect spot for leisurely gatherings and family outings.

**Tallinn Travel Guide**

**Alexander Nevsky Cathedral**

Marvel at the iconic Alexander Nevsky Cathedral, Tallinn's most renowned landmark. Built on the grounds where a pagan temple once stood, this cathedral dates back to 1240 and was originally constructed in gratitude for thwarting a Swedish invasion. The cathedral, completed in 1894, stands as a magnificent example of Russian church architecture. Inside, you'll discover ten captivating paintings by

Fyodor Rokotov and fourteen exquisite stained glass windows by Yevgeny Churygin. Outside, admire four striking sculptures by Mikhail Mikeshin representing the four evangelists: Matthew, Mark, Luke, and John.

## Hill of Angels

Experience the mystique of the Hill of Angels, steeped in legend and history. Encounter the echoes of the past as you wander this enigmatic site. By night, the hill comes alive with the laughter of youth, creating an atmosphere tinged with ghostly tales and modern adventures.

## Saint Mary's Cathedral:

Enter the Gothic masterpiece of Saint Mary's Cathedral, a beacon of medieval charm. Marvel at its exquisite stained glass windows and ascend the tower for panoramic views of the Old Town. Explore crypts, join a guided tour, and relish the unique ambiance of this historic gem.

## Song Festival Grounds

Discover the Song Festival Grounds, a historic Tallinn landmark where Estonians unite to celebrate their freedom. Situated in Tammsaare Park, this sprawling green space offers relaxation opportunities and picturesque settings for photos. Enjoy open-air concerts or watch children play on the playgrounds. Don't miss the lively 'Happiness Happens Here' festival, featuring dancing, live music, and artsy vendors. Nearby, the Lenin Monument offers breathtaking views of Toompea Hill.

## Maritime Museum

Step into the past at the Estonian Maritime Museum Association's Maritime Museum, established in 1936 on Kullassepa Street. As the oldest museum of its kind in Tallinn, it boasts a captivating collection. Explore model ships, shipyard models, maritime photographs, paintings, navigation aids, and artifacts from Estonian shipwrecks.

## Toompea Castle

Visit Toompea Castle, also known as Roccaa Al Mare Castle, perched atop Toompea Hill. This iconic castle has served as the Estonian government's seat since independence and ranks among Tallinn's top tourist attractions. From the central square, Freedom Square, enjoy panoramic views and marvel at the statue of Saint Christopher carrying Jesus across a river.

**KUMU Art Museum**

Immerse yourself in Estonian art at KUMU, one of Tallinn's most renowned museums, located on Raekoja Plats. Open Tuesday through Sunday, 11 a.m. to 6 p.m., KUMU offers a treasury of Estonian artistic treasures. Be sure to explore the café and restaurant with bay views. Notable exhibits include sculptures by Edward Krupp, paintings by Nikolai Triik, sculptural ceramics by Olav Neuland, and works by Mihkel Mutso. Don't miss the gallery showcasing their finest pieces.

## Museum of Occupations and Freedom Fights

Your journey through Tallinn isn't complete without a visit to the Museum of Occupations and Freedom Fights, Estonia's largest museum. Delve into history as it documents the period from 1940 to 1991, when Estonia was under Soviet occupation, and the relentless fight for independence that followed in 1991.

## Estonian Open Air Museum

Step back in time at the Estonian Open Air Museum, nestled within Haapsalu's former Manor Park. Roam through an expansive outdoor museum, where you can explore rustic farm buildings and traditional dwellings dating back to the pre-World War II era.

As your visit concludes, don't miss the chance to explore one of Estonia's beloved tourist attractions, Haapsalu Castle. This medieval gem from the 12th century boasts towers and other architectural wonders, offering a glimpse into castle life during the medieval era. Enhance your experience with a guided tour or immerse yourself further with an audio guide equipped with headphones, available in English, German, French, and Russian.

*Copyrighted Material*

# Recommended Hotels

Whether you're traveling with your family, as a couple, for a business trip, or looking for something budget-friendly, this travel guide has you covered.

**Citybox Tallinn: Ideal for Families**

When exploring Tallinn with your family, finding a central haven is key. The Citybox Hotel offers spacious, family-friendly rooms and convenient amenities. Located just 300 meters from Tallinn's heart, it's also pet-friendly! Nearby attractions like the Iron Game and Rotermann Quarter are within a stone's throw. Enjoy free high-speed internet, vending machines, and even table tennis. With various room types ranging from 11 to 35 square meters, choose what suits your needs. Most rooms boast air conditioning, flat-screen

TVs, and coffee machines. Prices vary based on room size and features.

## Hilton Tallinn Park: Perfect for Couples

For a romantic retreat, Hilton Tallinn Park beckons. Nestled 950 meters from Tallinn's center, it's a four-star haven near the Port of Tallinn. Enjoy stunning views and intimate spaces. Explore nearby gems like Up and Stockman. Indulge in free high-speed internet and unwind in the hotel's pool or fitness center. With 11 room types ranging from 32 to 80 square meters, find your ideal space. Rooms feature air conditioning, flat-screen TVs, and private bathrooms. Prices vary based on room size and amenities.

*Copyrighted Material*

## Hotel Meltzer Apartments: Ideal for Work Trips

For solo business travelers seeking convenience, Hotel Meltzer Apartments is your go-to choice. This 3.5-star gem is just 1.6 kilometers from Tallinn's center, offering proximity to the Vabamu Museum of Occupations and Freedom Square. Enjoy free high-speed internet, complimentary parking, Wi-Fi, a sauna, and even airport transportation. Choose from three room types ranging from 22 to 40 square meters. Most rooms feature air conditioning, private bathrooms, flat-screen TVs, mini-bars, and more. Prices vary based on room size and amenities.

## Tallink City Hotel: Luxury for Discerning Travelers

For those valuing both business and comfort, the four-star Tallink City Hotel is a top pick. Located a mere 250 meters from Tallinn's center, it offers easy access to Iron Game and the Estonian National Opera. Enjoy on-site parking, free high-speed internet, a sauna, and complimentary breakfast. With nine room types ranging from 17 to 55 square meters, find your perfect space. Most rooms include air conditioning, en-suite bathrooms, flat-screen TVs, and additional luxuries. Prices vary based on room size and amenities.

*Copyrighted Material*

## Center Hotel: Affordable and Convenient

Traveling on a budget? The Center Hotel is the perfect choice for cost-conscious travelers. Located just 750 meters from Tallinn's center, it offers easy access to local attractions like the Iron Game and escape rooms. Enjoy free high-speed internet, complimentary parking, and breakfast. With six room types ranging from 10 to 35 square meters, it's excellent value for money. Most rooms offer air conditioning, private bathrooms, flat-screen TVs, and convenient amenities. Prices vary based on room size and inclusions.

# Day Trip From Tallinn

## Day Trip from Tallinn to Lahemaa National Park

Just an hour's drive from the charming capital city of Tallinn lies a natural wonder waiting to be explored. Lahemaa National Park, Estonia's oldest and largest national park, is a haven of pristine forests, rugged coastlines, and cultural heritage. Join us on a one-day adventure as we escape the city and dive into the beauty of Lahemaa.

Morning:

Begin your journey early in the morning from Tallinn, either by car or by taking a convenient bus.

Enjoy a picturesque hour-long drive through the countryside en route to Lahemaa.

Stop 1: Palmse Manor

Commence your day at Palmse Manor, an elegant 18th-century estate. Explore the grand mansion and beautiful gardens, and delve into Estonia's aristocratic history.

Stroll through the French-style park and uncover captivating tales of the estate.

### Stop 2: Sagadi Manor

Next, head to Sagadi Manor, another historical gem nestled in the park. Explore the manor house, now a museum dedicated to Estonian forests and nature.

Take a leisurely walk along the nature trail to immerse yourself in Lahemaa's natural beauty.

### Lunch:

Enjoy a picnic amidst the park's tranquility or savor traditional Estonian cuisine at a local restaurant.

### Afternoon:

Drive to Altja, a charming fishing village preserving Estonia's coastal traditions. Explore picturesque wooden houses and visit the fishing museum.

Choose from various coastal hiking trails offering stunning views of the Baltic Sea and Lahemaa forest.

Stop 4: Viru Bog Boardwalk

Experience the ethereal beauty of Viru Bog by walking along the boardwalk. This ancient peat bog is home to unique flora and fauna.

Don't forget your camera; the landscape is perfect for capturing Estonia's natural wonders.

Evening:

As the day winds down, make your way back to Tallinn, reminiscing about the day's adventures.

Treat yourself to a delicious dinner at one of Tallinn's many restaurants, reflecting on your unforgettable day in Lahemaa National Park.

*Copyrighted Material*

A day trip from Tallinn to Lahemaa National Park offers a delightful escape into Estonia's natural and cultural heritage. With a mix of history, stunning landscapes, and coastal beauty, Lahemaa promises an enriching experience for every traveler. So, when you're in Tallinn, take a day off to explore the wonders of Lahemaa National Park.

## Day Trip From Tallinn To Pärnu

Escape the bustling energy of Tallinn and embark on a blissful day trip to Pärnu, Estonia's picturesque seaside town. Just a few hours from the capital, Pärnu invites you to unwind on its golden beaches and immerse yourself in coastal charm. Let's craft a perfect day for you!

**Morning:**

Begin your day early at Tallinn's central bus station. Relax on a comfortable 2.5-hour bus ride, enjoying the scenic Estonian countryside.

Arrive in the heart of town and head straight to the stunning Pärnu Beach. Its soft sands and shallow waters create a perfect oasis for a morning swim.

**Midday:**

Lunch at Ammende Villa: Indulge in elegance at Ammende Villa. This historical gem offers exquisite Estonian cuisine in a refined atmosphere. Delight in local delicacies for a true culinary experience.

**Afternoon:**

Take a leisurely stroll through the charming old town. Marvel at the well-preserved Hanseatic architecture, colorful buildings, and winding streets. Don't miss the iconic Red Tower and the lively Town Hall Square.

Immerse yourself in the local art scene at Pärnu Museum or the contemporary Pärnu New Art Museum. Both venues provide captivating glimpses into the town's rich history and modern artistic expressions.

Late Afternoon:

Seek serenity in Rannapark, a peaceful green space along the Pärnu River. Capture moments, unwind, or enjoy a tranquil picnic by the water's edge.

Evening:

Conclude your day with a delightful meal at a waterfront restaurant like Steffani Pizzarestoran. Relish mouthwatering dishes while the sun paints the sky with vibrant hues over the horizon.

As the day draws to a close, carry the serenity and charm of Pärnu back to Tallinn with you. While this day trip offers just a glimpse of Pärnu's allure, it will undoubtedly leave you longing for more. Estonia's coastal gem promises relaxation, culture, and a touch of seaside magic, all easily accessible from Tallinn.

**Copyrighted Material**

## Day Trip from Tallinn to Tartu

Commence your journey in Estonia's vibrant capital, Tallinn, and embark on an exhilarating day trip to the enchanting city of Tartu. This guide will whirl you through Tartu's highlights, providing valuable tips and insights to enhance your day.

Morning:

Start your day early by catching a comfortable express bus or train from Tallinn to Tartu. The journey, lasting around 2.5 to 3 hours, offers picturesque vistas of Estonia's countryside.

Dive into Tartu's academic legacy with a visit to the Tartu University Museum. Discover the institution's profound influence on Estonia's intellectual evolution.

Wander through Toome Hill Park, where the captivating ruins of the Tartu Cathedral await. Revel in the serene ambiance and relish panoramic views of the city.

Lunch:

Lunch at a Local Café

Head to Tartu's town center for a delectable lunch experience. Choose from a myriad of local cafes and restaurants, offering Estonian delicacies and international flavors.

Afternoon:

Immerse yourself in Estonian culture at the Estonian National Museum. Explore captivating exhibits, folk traditions, and the nation's vibrant history.

Continue your artistic odyssey at the Tartu Art Museum, a showcase of contemporary and classical Estonian artistry.

Late Afternoon:

Embark on a leisurely walk along the picturesque Emajõgi River, where you can bask in the tranquil scenery and, if you desire, partake in a serene boat ride.

Evening:

Dinner at a Local Eatery:

For your evening repast, indulge in a local restaurant or tavern offering Estonian specialties and global cuisine.

Explore the charming alleys of Tartu's Old Town, renowned for its cobblestone pathways and historic edifices.

As the curtain falls on your day in Tartu, embark on your journey back to Tallinn, reminiscing about the cultural treasures and delightful encounters that have adorned your day in this splendid Estonian city.

This day trip provides a tantalizing glimpse into Tartu's history, culture, and natural allure, enhancing your Estonian adventure with indelible memories. Enjoy your exploration of Tartu!

*Copyrighted Material*

# Your 5-Day Itinerary

## DAY 1

MORNING:

Begin your day with a delightful cup of coffee at Kohvik Must Puudel. Then, step back in time in Tallinn's Old Town. Wander the cobblestone streets, marvel at the historic architecture, and soak in the panoramic views from Toompea Hill.

AFTERNOON:

Indulge in Estonian cuisine at Rataskaevu 16 for lunch. Explore Kadriorg Palace and its picturesque gardens. Art enthusiasts can't miss the KUMU Art Museum nearby, which showcases Estonia's vibrant artistic heritage.

EVENING:

Savor an authentic Estonian dinner at Olde Hansa, a medieval-themed restaurant offering a unique culinary experience. Afterward, take a leisurely stroll down lively Viru Street. Explore charming local shops and boutiques, immersing yourself in Tallinn's vibrant evening ambiance.

BEDTIME:

Head back to your cozy hotel in Tallinn, where you can unwind and prepare for the adventures that await on Day 2 of your Tallinn exploration.

## DAY 2

MORNING:

Start your day with a visit to the Tallinn TV Tower, which offers panoramic views of the city. Afterward, enjoy a quick breakfast at Restoran Platz before heading to the Seaplane Harbour. Dive into Estonia's maritime history and even step inside a real submarine.

AFTERNOON:

For lunch, venture to F-Hoone, a trendy restaurant located in a former industrial space. After your meal, explore the Telliskivi Creative City, a dynamic neighborhood filled with art galleries, boutiques, and cozy cafes. Don't miss the chance to peruse local design shops.

EVENING:

Indulge in a sumptuous dinner at Noa, a Michelin-starred restaurant renowned for its innovative Nordic cuisine. Following your meal, make your way to the Kultuurikatel for an evening of culture. Check their schedule for live performances, concerts, or other engaging events.

BEDTIME:

Return to your comfortable Tallinn hotel for a peaceful night's rest, recharging for another exciting day ahead in this modern and vibrant city.

## Day 3

**MORNING:**

Begin your day with a visit to Kadriorg Park, a serene oasis filled with picturesque landscapes and enchanting walking paths. Take a leisurely morning stroll, immersing yourself in the natural beauty. Afterward, savor a light breakfast at Balti Jaama Turg.

**AFTERNOON:**

For lunch, make your way to Farm and relish their farm-to-table dishes crafted from locally sourced ingredients. Post-meal, venture to the Tallinn Botanic Garden, where diverse plant collections await. Allow yourself to unwind and bask in the garden's tranquility.

**EVENING:**

Pamper yourself with a spa evening at Grand Rose Spa, indulging in rejuvenating treatments and relaxation. Afterward, savor a delectable dinner at Leib Resto ja Aed, a restaurant celebrated for its modern Estonian cuisine.

BEDTIME:

Conclude your day in Tallinn with a restful night's sleep at your chosen hotel. Recharge for whatever adventures the following day may bring.

## Day 4

MORNING:

Start your day with a visit to the Estonian Open Air Museum. Discover Estonian rural life and traditions as you wander among authentic buildings and engaging exhibits. Following your exploration, enjoy a quick breakfast at Rotermann Quarter.

AFTERNOON:

lunch, delight in the offerings at Poestkook, a cozy cafe serving an array of delightful pastries and sandwiches. Afterward, delve into Estonia's history during the Soviet occupation at the KGB Museum. Enhance your understanding with a guided tour that offers profound insights into the nation's past.

**EVENING:**

Savor a traditional Estonian dinner at Von Krahli Aed, a restaurant celebrated for its rustic ambiance and hearty cuisine. Following your meal, venture to Viru Keskus, a shopping center housing a blend of international and local brands. Take your time exploring the shops or catching a film at the cinema.

**BEDTIME:**

As the day comes to an end, return to your chosen Tallinn hotel for a peaceful night's sleep. Rest well, preparing for more enriching experiences on your journey through Tallinn, Estonia.

## DAY 5

MORNING:

Embark on a day trip to Tartu, Estonia's second-largest city. Commence your day with a visit to the University of Tartu, one of Northern Europe's oldest universities. Delve into the historic campus and its charming surroundings. Grab a quick breakfast at Werner Cafe.

AFTERNOON:

For lunch, savor the offerings at Truffe, a cozy restaurant known for its variety of European dishes. Afterward, venture to the AHHAA Science Center, where interactive exhibits and scientific experiments await your exploration.

EVENING:

Return to Tallinn and relish a farewell dinner at Restoran Ö. Delight in their innovative tasting menu, savoring the rich flavors of Estonian cuisine. Following your meal, take a leisurely stroll along the Tallinn City Wall, enjoying the city's illuminated landmarks.

BEDTIME:

As your day of adventure and exploration comes to an end, retire to your chosen Tallinn hotel for a night of reflection and rest. Prepare to bid farewell to this captivating city with a heart full of memories.

## Conclusion

As we conclude our journey through the captivating streets of Tallinn, you may find yourself torn between the anticipation of future adventures and the bittersweet moment of parting with a city that has touched your heart. Tallinn, with its timeless beauty and rich history, has a unique way of leaving an indelible mark on those who meander through its cobblestone lanes and embrace its warm hospitality.

Throughout our exploration, you've delved into the annals of history within the medieval walls of Old Town, where tales of merchants and knights whispered in the breeze. You've savored the flavors of Estonia in cozy cafes and fine dining establishments, relishing traditional dishes that tell tales of generations. You've wandered through the charming neighborhoods of Kadriorg and Kalamaja, uncovering hidden gems and artistic inspirations around every corner.

However, Tallinn is more than just a compilation of historic sites and cultural treasures; it's a city of contrasts. While you marveled at the modern skyline, you witnessed a place that embraces the future with innovation and ambition. Tallinn effortlessly melds the old and the new, crafting a unique destination that caters to diverse tastes and interests.

As we bid adieu to Tallinn, I encourage you to carry with you the memories of its enchantment—the laughter shared with locals, the mesmerizing sunsets over the Baltic Sea, and the friendships forged along the way. The experiences you've amassed in this remarkable city are not merely stories to recount; they are integral threads in the tapestry of your own life's journey.

As you turn the final pages of this guide, remember that Tallinn will always welcome you back with open arms. Whether you return to rediscover familiar corners or seek new adventures, Tallinn will remain a city of boundless opportunities, ready to craft new stories and cherished memories. Until then, may your travels be imbued with wonder, discovery, and the enduring spirit of adventure.

Farewell, dear traveler, and may your next destination be as unforgettable as Tallinn, Estonia.

# Tallinn Travel Planner

**This Journal belongs to:**

_____

**Contact Address:**

_____

_____

# TRAVEL ITINERARY

**DAY 1**

**DAY 2**

**DAY 3**

**DAY 4**

*Copyrighted Material*

# TRAVEL ITINERARY

DAY 5

DAY 6

DAY 7

# Travel Bucket List

| PLACES TO VISIT | THINGS I WANT TO DO |
|---|---|
|  |  |
|  |  |
|  |  |
|  |  |

| FOODS TO TASTE | PRODUCTS TO BUY |
|---|---|
|  |  |
|  |  |
|  |  |
|  |  |

# Travel Bucket List

## PLACES TO VISIT

## THINGS I WANT TO DO

## FOODS TO TASTE

## PRODUCTS TO BUY

# Travel Bucket List

| PLACES TO VISIT | THINGS I WANT TO DO |
|---|---|
| | |

| FOODS TO TASTE | PRODUCTS TO BUY |
|---|---|
| | |

# PACKING LIST

**Clothing**
- _____
- _____
- _____
- _____
- _____
- _____
- _____
- _____

**Electronic & Gadgets**
- _____
- _____
- _____
- _____
- _____
- _____
- _____
- _____

**Toiletries**
- _____
- _____
- _____
- _____
- _____
- _____
- _____
- _____

**Accessories**
- _____
- _____
- _____
- _____
- _____
- _____
- _____
- _____

**Health**
- _____
- _____
- _____
- _____
- _____

**Essentials**
- _____
- _____
- _____
- _____
- _____

# PACKING LIST

**Clothing**
- 
- 
- 
- 
- 
- 
- 
- 

**Electronic & Gadgets**
- 
- 
- 
- 
- 
- 
- 
- 

**Toiletries**
- 
- 
- 
- 
- 
- 
- 
- 

**Accessories**
- 
- 
- 
- 
- 
- 
- 
- 

**Health**
- 
- 
- 
- 
- 
- 

**Essentials**
- 
- 
- 
- 
- 
-

# PACKING LIST

**Clothing**
- _____
- _____
- _____
- _____
- _____
- _____
- _____
- _____

**Electronic & Gadgets**
- _____
- _____
- _____
- _____
- _____
- _____
- _____
- _____

**Toiletries**
- _____
- _____
- _____
- _____
- _____
- _____
- _____
- _____

**Accessories**
- _____
- _____
- _____
- _____
- _____
- _____
- _____
- _____

**Health**
- _____
- _____
- _____
- _____
- _____

**Essentials**
- _____
- _____
- _____
- _____
- _____

# PACKING LIST

### Clothing
○ _____
○ _____
○ _____
○ _____
○ _____
○ _____
○ _____

### Electronic & Gadgets
○ _____
○ _____
○ _____
○ _____
○ _____
○ _____
○ _____

### Toiletries
○ _____
○ _____
○ _____
○ _____
○ _____
○ _____
○ _____

### Accessories
○ _____
○ _____
○ _____
○ _____
○ _____
○ _____
○ _____

### Health
○ _____
○ _____
○ _____
○ _____
○ _____

### Essentials
○ _____
○ _____
○ _____
○ _____
○ _____

# TO DO LIST

MONTH

DATE

## TO DO

- [ ] ----
- [ ] ----
- [ ] ----
- [ ] ----
- [ ] ----
- [ ] ----
- [ ] ----
- [ ] ----
- [ ] ----
- [ ] ----
- [ ] ----
- [ ] ----
- [ ] ----
- [ ] ----
- [ ] ----
- [ ] ----
- [ ] ----
- [ ] ----

## PRIORITIES

- [ ] ----
- [ ] ----
- [ ] ----
- [ ] ----
- [ ] ----
- [ ] ----
- [ ] ----

## NOTES

## REMINDER

# TO DO LIST

**MONTH**

**DATE**

**TO DO**
- [ ] _____
- [ ] _____
- [ ] _____
- [ ] _____
- [ ] _____
- [ ] _____
- [ ] _____
- [ ] _____
- [ ] _____
- [ ] _____
- [ ] _____
- [ ] _____
- [ ] _____
- [ ] _____
- [ ] _____
- [ ] _____
- [ ] _____
- [ ] _____

**PRIORITIES**
- [ ] _____
- [ ] _____
- [ ] _____
- [ ] _____
- [ ] _____
- [ ] _____
- [ ] _____

**NOTES**

**REMINDER**

*Copyrighted Material*

# TO DO LIST

MONTH

DATE

TO DO

PRIORITIES

NOTES

REMINDER

# My Notes

# My Notes

# My Notes

# My Notes

# My Notes

# My Notes

------

------

------

------

------

------

------

------

# My Notes

# My Notes

# My Notes

Printed in Great Britain
by Amazon